TOM
THE DANCING BUG

A COLLECTION OF CARTOONS BY
RUBEN BOLLING

HarperPerennial
A Division of HarperCollinsPublishers

HarperCollins books may be purchased for educational, business, or sales promotional use. For information please write: Special Markets Department, HarperCollins Publishers, Inc., 10 East 53rd Street, New York, NY 10022.

FIRST EDITION

Designed by George J. McKeon

ISBN 0-06-096949-0

92 93 94 95 96 ❖RRD 10 9 8 7 6 5 4 3 2 1

THE PARTY WAS GOING **WELL** UNTIL THE AUSTRALO-PITHECINE SHOWED UP.

CHARLEY'S OFFERING TO THE HOSTESS IS UNAPPRECIATED.

SCHAEFER-LIGHT TALL-BOYS?

ENJOY!

CONVERSATION IS NOT SMOOTH.

ANYBODY WANT TO SEE MY CANKER SORE?

BOASTS ABOUT HIS METHOD OF LOCOMOTION ARE WHOLLY MISUNDERSTOOD.

DON'T GET ME WRONG-- I'M NO HOMO-ERECTUS OR ANYTHING, BUT I AM FULLY BIPEDAL.

LIBERTIES ARE TAKEN.

SORRY I WAS SO LONG. WHEN I SAW THEY HAD A "WET TUNES", I COULDN'T RESIST A SHOWER.

AFTER A TERRITORIAL DISPLAY WHEN SOMEONE APPROACHES THE CHEEZ-DOODLES...

RAARRRR!

...AND AN UNFORTUNATE SCHAEFER-LIGHT-INDUCED EPISODE...

THE WATER BUFFALO ARE ON THE RUN! **HIT THE DECK!**

NO, I THOUGHT **YOU** IN-VITED HIM!

...THE EVENING COMES TO AN ABRUPT END.

SLAM!

4B

MAN, WAS I A HIT!

Suddenly, an insignificant territorial squabble between troops of hamadryas baboons assumed global significance when it was revealed that one of the troops had inexplicably attained nuclear technology.

TOM THE DANCING BUG

HELLO, AND WELCOME TO "MUTUAL OF NEBRASKA'S WILD KINGDOM." TODAY WE SET OUT TO SEE HOW A RADICAL CHANGE IN THE ENVIRONMENT WILL AFFECT ONE OF NATURE'S MOST ABUNDANT SPECIES.

WE HEAD DOWNTOWN AMONG THE CANYONS OF NEW YORK CITY IN SEARCH OF...

THE TAX LAWYER!

SOME SAY THAT CHANGES IN "THE TAX CODE"--THE TAX LAWYER'S FOOD SOURCE--WILL CAUSE A DRASTIC REDUCTION IN THEIR NUMBERS. OTHERS ACTUALLY PREDICT AN INCREASE!

UH-OH! JIM'S SPOTTED ONE ALREADY!

IT'S A LONE MALE. WE'RE LUCKY-- THEY USUALLY TRAVEL IN PACKS!

THE CHOPPER HAS STARTLED HIM, AND HE'S ON THE MOVE! THEY'VE BEEN CLOCKED AT SIX MILES AN HOUR IN A FULL SPRINT, SO JIM WILL HAVE TO AIM CAREFULLY...

POW!

GOT HIM!!

THE TRANQUILIZER'S EFFECT WILL LAST A FEW MOMENTS--ENOUGH TO TAG HIM AND PUT ON A TRANSMITTING DEVICE. THIS WILL PROVIDE VALUABLE INFORMATION ABOUT HIS MIGRATION AND MATING HABITS.

THE BIG FELLA'S AWAKENING NOW...

beep beep

AND HE'S ON HIS WAY--NONE THE WORSE FOR THE EXPERIENCE.

beep beep beep

THIS RESEARCH WILL HELP DETERMINE EXACTLY WHAT EFFECT A CHANGE IN TAX LAWS WILL HAVE ON THIS SPECIES. ONE THING, HOWEVER, IS CERTAIN: WE MUST LEARN THAT WE CANNOT INDISCRIMINATELY TAMPER WITH THE LEGAL ENVIRONMENT FOR OUR OWN SELFISH ENDS. WE MUST REMEMBER THAT WE SHARE THE EARTH WITH OTHER CREATURES-- SUCH AS THE MAJESTIC *TAX LAWYER!*

©1991 RUBEN BOLLING

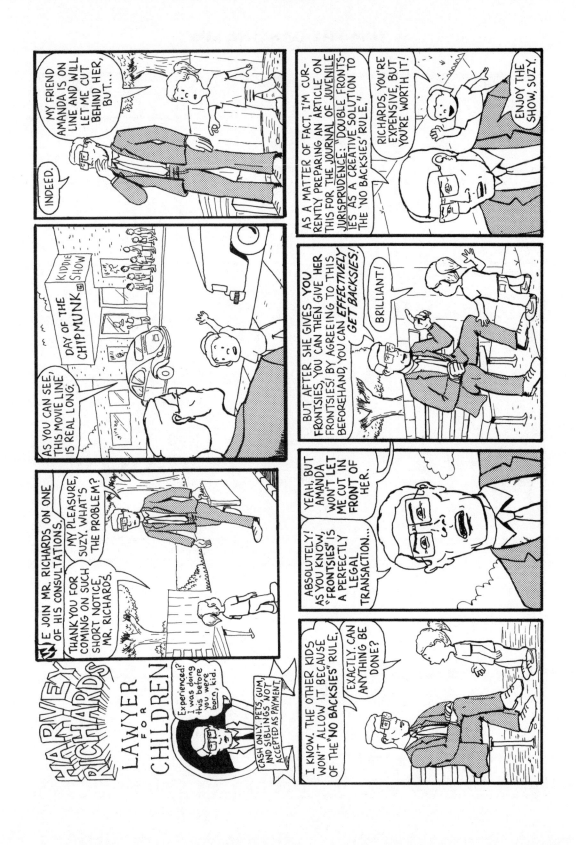

WHEN THEIR DIVERSE PERSONALITIES AND TALENTS ARE BROUGHT TOGETHER, THEY CAN DO THE **IMPOSSIBLE!!**

THEY'RE-- **THE IMPOSSIBLE SQUAD!** ©1991 ROOTIN' RUBEN BOLLING

SGT. MAC HARDY
DOUBLE-FISTED, NAILS-EATING POWERHOUSE!
SPECIALTY: EXPLOSIVES

SGT. ROCK RUMBLE
BARREL-CHESTED, HOT-HEADED TOUGH GUY!
SPECIALTY: EXPLOSIVES

SGT. NICK WYLDE
HARD-NOSED, GUTSY DOUBLE-FLUSHER!
SPECIALTY: EXPLOSIVES

SGT. KURT STEELE
HEAVYWEIGHT, FISTS FLYIN' HOT SHOT!
SPECIALTY: EXPLOSIVES

SGT. JACK DUKES
CIGAR-CHOMPING, HULKING STEAMROLLER!
SPECIALTY: ENTOMOLOGY

OKAY, YOU PALOOKAS, LISTEN UP! HERE'S THE MISSION: WE GOTTA TAKE OUT THIS SUPPLY BRIDGE! ANY BRIGHT IDEAS?

I SAY WE GO WIT' EXPLOSIVES! LET'S BLOW THAT SUCKER TO *PEORIA!!*

YEAH, THAT LOUSY BRIDGE AIN'T NOTHIN' SOME GOOD OL' *TNT* CAN'T HANDLE!

YEAH!

NOW, HOLD YER STOGIES!! I GOT A BETTER IDEA! I SAY WE USE...

TERMITES!!

AW, DUKES! NOT AGAIN...!

SURE! WE JUST LET A FEW THOUSAND *ISOPTERAS* LOOSE AND WATCH THE FUN! IN A FEW MONTHS, THOSE BABIES...

THAT DOES IT, DUKES!! I'VE **HAD** IT WIT' YER BLASTED BUGS! IT'S ALWAYS **ANTS** THIS, AN' **BEES** THAT! I'M GONNA SQUASH YOU FER GOOD!!

I'M READY, STEELE! LET'S SEE YA TRY!

ALRIGHT! COOL YER JETS, STEELE! YA **KNOW** THAT ENTO-MOLOGY IS DUKES'S SPECIALTY!

AH, SARGE! IT'S A CONCRETE BRIDGE, FER CRYIN' OUT LOUD!

NEXT: BATTLIN' BUGS!!

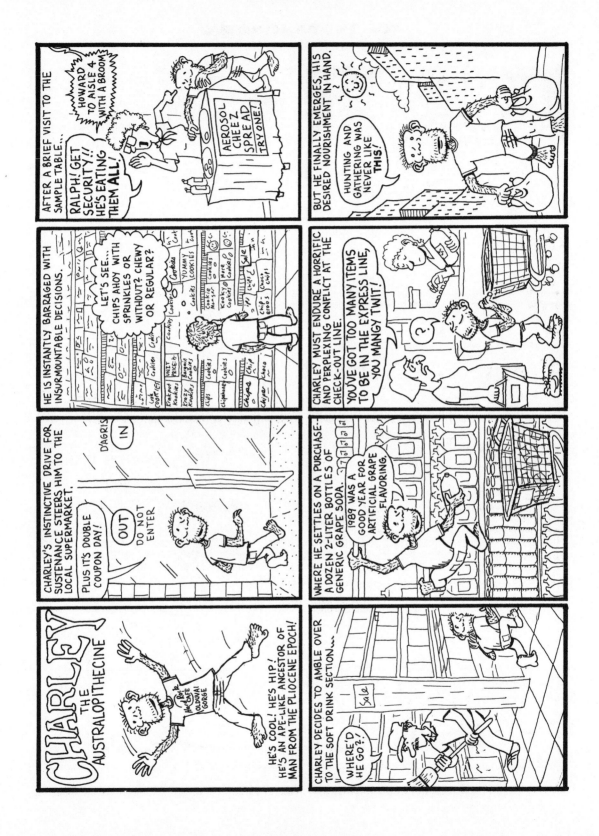

ADVANCES in sitcom TECHNOLOGY

EVERYONE IS WELL AWARE OF THE RECENT TECHNOLOGICAL LEAPS MADE IN THE FIELDS OF TELECOMMUNICATIONS, GLOBAL WEAPONRY AND GOLF BALL PRODUCTION. HOWEVER, THE STARTLING ADVANCES IN SITCOM TECHNOLOGY HAVE GONE LARGELY UNNOTICED. HERE WE SALUTE THE ACCOMPLISHMENTS OF THE MEN AND WOMEN WHO HAVE DEVOTED THEIR LIVES TO FURTHERING THIS SCIENCE.

IN THE 1960's, SITCOMS LANGUISHED IN A PRIMITIVE STAGE, USING SIMPLE LAUGH-TRACKS.

THAT'S JUST WHAT THE CAPTAIN OF THE **TITANIC** SAID!

H GUFFAW! YEE HA! HA! HO! HAW!

DOUG as a wacky neighbor

IN THE 1970's, THE FIRST BREAK-THROUGH OCCURRED. RESEARCH SCIENTISTS WORKING FOR "GOOD TIMES" DEVELOPED THE FIRST OO-TRACK. ITS USE IS NOW COMMONPLACE.

THE RUNAWAY SUCCESS OF THE OO-TRACK LED TO A FLURRY OF NEW AUDIENCE-SIMULATION TRACKS (ASTs). AMONG THE MOST PREVALENT ARE THE AW-TRACK...

LISTEN UP, **PENCIL NECK!**

OOO! OOO! OOOO! OO!

I'M SORRY. I WAS ONLY TRYING TO HELP! I LOVE YOU **SO MUCH!**

AWWW! AW! AW! AW! AW!

MAX as a precocious but endearing child

...AND THE NEWEST ADDITION, THE COLLECTIVE-GASP-TRACK.

GENIUS SCOTT BAIO HAS REVOLUTIONIZED THE USE OF ASTs BY RUNNING ALL FOUR CONTINUOUSLY THROUGHOUT HIS MASTERWORK SITCOM, "CHARLES IN CHARGE."

I STOLE THE MONEY... TO TEACH YOU ALL A **LESSON!**

GASP!

© 1990 Ruben Bolling

BUDDY, IF YOU WERE ANY DUMBER, YOU'D BE A **DOORKNOB!**

HA! GASP! HAW! AW! OOO!

Next Week: WHEN SITCOM SCIENTISTS DISCOVER SPLIT-SCREEN TECHNIQUES, THE IDENTICAL COUSIN CONCEPT IS BORN, AND THE FACE OF HUMOR IS CHANGED FOREVER!

the claus view
part 1

©1990 RUBEN BOLLING

I WANT TO THANK YOU FOR SEEING ME. I KNOW A LOT OF THE THINGS I SAID ON THE PHONE MUST HAVE SOUNDED CRAZY. I COULDN'T BELIEVE IT MY-SELF, AT FIRST. NOW I KNOW...

I'M IN GREAT DANGER JUST BEING HERE. BUT WHAT I HAVE TO TELL YOU-- THE **TRUTH**--HAS TO GET OUT! PEOPLE HAVE TO KNOW!

WHERE DO I BEGIN? WELL, AT THE BEGINNING, I GUESS.

It was last month, December, that it started. It was a time of wonder -- of snow-white optimism.

I was like any other kid, I suppose. I loved Christmas. And Santa Claus. What kid doesn't love him? Hell, I even had my list -- I wanted a soccer ball and a G.I. Joe Desert Action Gift Set. And if I was good, Santa would bring them. Yeah. Right.

I guess I first noticed that something was wrong one day in town. Ah, maybe that's a lie. Maybe I knew something was wrong all the time -- just didn't admit it to myself.

VISIT SANTA

Seeing several different Santas in the same day was no revelation. I'd always believed the standard explanation: that these are not the "real" Santas, they are Santa's helpers.

For some reason, that just didn't wash this year. I needed to know more.

MOM? ARE SANTA'S HELPERS FROM THE NORTH POLE LIKE SANTA?

YES, DEAR. UM, THEY ALL LIVE AT THE NORTH POLE WITH SANTA, AND AT CHRIST-MASTIME, THEY COME DOWN TO THE TOWNS AND CITIES.

Well, this just didn't seem to make sense. I couldn't picture countless Santa-look-a-likes all living together for eleven months a year, waiting for Christmas-time. This isn't the picture of the North Pole you see on T.V. A pit of doubt formed deep in my stomach.

Next week: A startling confrontation!

the claus view
part II

©1990 RUBEN BOLLING

THAT'S WHEN I BEGAN TO REALIZE THAT THE SANTA STORY I WAS BEING TOLD JUST DIDN'T ADD UP!

The more I thought about it, the more rotten it all seemed. If those guys I saw in the stores and on the street weren't really Santa's helpers, who **were** they?

Countless questions swam in my mind: What were these imposters trying to accomplish? And, even more importantly, **Who else knew?**

That Saturday, I went back to the department store to see the Santa.

On his break, I followed him to the employee's lounge.

I watched in wide-eyed terror as "Santa" shed his trappings -- revealing an ordinary, middle-aged bald guy!

The horror of the scene spurred a sudden boldness within me, and I found myself confronting him!

HEY! YOU'RE NOT REALLY A SANTA! YOU'RE A REGULAR GUY DRESSED UP!

YEAH, THAT'S RIGHT, KID. I AIN'T NO SANTA. THE STORE PAYS ME TO PUT ON THIS GET-UP AND IT'S HO-HO-HO ALL DAY. THE JOB'S GOOD FOR EXTRA BOOZE MONEY.

B-BUT ALL THOSE KIDS WHO BELIEVE! DOES ...DOES THE REAL SANTA KNOW YOU'RE DOING THIS?!

KID, DON'T ASK ANY QUESTIONS YOU DON'T WANT TO KNOW THE ANSWERS TO! NOW, IF YOU KNOW WHAT'S GOOD FOR YOU, YOU'LL RUN HOME AND FORGET YOU EVER SAW THIS!

Next week: How deep do the murky waters of conspiracy run? My worst fears realized!

the claus view
part III

©1990 RUBEN BOLLING

Christmas Eve: While other kids were blissfully dreaming about dancing plums and crap like that, I was crouched in a dark closet, my mind reeling.

I had discovered that the department store Santas were fakes! I had to know who else was in on the insidious conspiracy. The television networks? The Mafia? The Communists? The CIA?

Most importantly, I had to know if the **real** Santa knew about it.

Suddenly, I heard muffled sounds in the living room. I knew it was time... I swung the door open!

NO! NO! **NO!**

MOM! DAD! NOT YOU TOO!!

Their shocked faces told it all. My world crumbled before my eyes. The corruption was complete.

AND SO I'VE COME TO YOU. YOU'VE GOT TO PUBLISH MY STORY--TO TELL KIDS EVERYWHERE OF THIS HIDEOUS CONSPIRACY DESIGNED TO KEEP THEM IGNORANT OF THE TRUTH-- THAT THERE IS **NO SANTA CLAUS!**

KID, WE JUST PUBLISH PUZZLES AND STORIES FOR CHILDREN. I'M NOT GOING TO PRINT A STORY ABOUT A SANTA CONSPIRACY!

SO THE PRESS IS IN ON THE COVER-UP TOO? I SUSPECTED AS MUCH! WELL, I'LL GET MY STORY OUT-- EVEN IF I HAVE TO SCREAM MY MESSAGE ON THE STREETS!

As I left the office, I could swear I could hear hollow, mocking laughter echoing in the halls.

HO, HO, HO!

The end.

AN AUSTRALO-PITHECINE WALKS AMONG US!

SHOCKING BUT TRUE! THERE HAVE BEEN NUMEROUS SIGHTINGS OF AN AUSTRALOPITHECINE IN OUR FAIR CITY!

ARTIST'S RENDERING

THE ONLY PHOTO OF THIS CREATURE IS THIS SHOT FROM A SECURITY CAMERA IN A 7-11. AN ANALYSIS HAS REVEALED THAT IT

WAS PURCHASING A GRAPE SODA BIG GULP AND THREE SNICKERS BARS.

WHAT IS AN AUSTRALOPITHECINE? IT IS AN APE-LIKE CREATURE THAT LIVED 3½ MILLION YEARS AGO. AS YOU CAN SEE FROM THIS CHART, IT IS AN ANCESTOR OF HUMANITY.

FISH WITH FEET

AUSTRALO-PITHECINE

CRO-MAGNON MAN

ANCHOR MAN

A NOTED SCIENTIST: DIS AUSTRALOPICOLO IS DER BEAST VROM VHICH CIVILIZED MAN EMERGED. VHILE VE HAFF SOCIETAL NORMS TO INHIBIT OUR IMPULSES, HE ACTS ON HIS EVERY URGE, JA? IN SHORT, HE IS A VALKING ID!

WE ASKED SOME PASSERSBY WHAT THEY THINK:

I THINK WE SHOULD HUNT THE FILTHY THING DOWN AND BLOW ITS BRAINS OUT.

WE OUGHT TO CAPTURE IT AND USE IT FOR RESEARCH--YOU KNOW, LIKE TEST COSMETICS ON IT.

UM... I THINK WE SHOULD GIVE IT GRAPE SODA AND FREE CABLE.

NEXT UP: A MAN WHO CLAIMS TO HAVE SEEN THE AUSTRALOPITHECINE ATTACK A VANLOAD OF NUNS.

NOT A AUSTROPO LITHPIKY!.. ELVIS!!

HEY, KIDS!

© 1990 Ruben Bolling

GET YOUR CENTRAL PARK __SOFTBALL TRADING CARDS!__

HERE ARE YOUR FAVORITE PLAYERS FROM THE WEEKEND PICK-UP GAMES ON THE HALLOWED FIELDS OF CENTRAL PARK!

HEY, I'LL TRADE YOU MY JOEL PALMER FOR YOUR FRANK JACKSON.

A LOUSY STEREO SALESMAN FOR AN INVESTMENT BANKER?! NO WAY!!

COLLECT 'EM! TRADE 'EM! FLIP 'EM!

JUST CUT OUT THE CARDS AND FOLD 'EM OVER!

MARK HANNISH
NICKNAME: "THAT JERK IN THE HAT"

MARK IS FAMOUS THROUGHOUT THE PARK FOR HIS LOUD AND ESOTERIC ARGUMENTS!

FUN FACT: AFTER EACH OF HIS MANY AND FREQUENT ERRORS, MARK MAKES SURE TO CURSE LOUDLY SO THAT EVERYONE UNDERSTANDS THAT HE CONSIDERS IT AN ABERRATIONAL EVENT!

QUOTE: "GET THAT LOSER OUT OF CENTERFIELD!"

HECTOR MARTIN
NICKNAME: "JOSE CANSECO"

HECTOR IS ABLE TO KEEP HIS AUTHENTIC BASEBALL UNIFORM IN IMMACULATE CONDITION BY NEVER GETTING ON BASE.

FUN FACT: HECTOR SAYS HE WILL NOT ALLOW HIS ONGOING RECORD OF 147 CONSECUTIVE FLY OUTS TO DEEP LEFTFIELD AFFECT HIS BATTING STYLE!

QUOTE: "AT LEAST I'M NOT GETTING THOSE WIMPY GROUNDBALL SINGLES."

PETER ZANNI
NICKNAME: "HEY, YOU!"

PETE'S SOLE APPEARANCE THIS SEASON OCCURRED WHEN HE WAS CROSSING THE PARK AND WAS CALLED OVER BECAUSE A TEAM NEEDED A NINTH PLAYER. "UM, OKAY," WAS HIS ENTHUSIASTIC RESPONSE.

FUN FACT: HEAVY, BLACK ARMY BOOTS ARE THE ONLY ATHLETIC FOOTWEAR FOR PETE!

QUOTE: "CAN I BORROW YOUR GLOVE?"

I TRY TO BE A GOOD PERSON. I WANT TO DO WHAT'S RIGHT.

I DON'T GIVE MONEY DIRECTLY TO STREET PEOPLE BECAUSE I FEEL IT'S BETTER TO GIVE IT TO AGENCIES THAT AID THE HOMELESS.

OTHER THAN THAT, I TRY TO BE A GOOD SAMARITAN-- HELP WHEN I CAN.

SO ANYWAY, I'M OUT THE OTHER NIGHT, AND THIS GUY COMES UP TO ME AND SAYS, "CAN YOU HELP ME OUT? I JUST NEED 25 MORE CENTS, AND I CAN BUY A SUBWAY TOKEN."

I'M LOOKING AT HIM, TRYING TO DECIDE WHO HE IS-- WHETHER HE'S A STREET PERSON TRYING TO SCAM ME, OR IF HE'S REALLY A REGULAR GUY IN TROUBLE...

AND SUDDENLY I REALIZE-- I'M TRYING TO FIGURE OUT IF HE JUST NEEDS MONEY TO GET ON THE SUBWAY, IN WHICH CASE I'LL GIVE IT TO HIM...

OR IF HE'S DESPERATELY POOR AND NEEDS THE MONEY FOR SURVIVAL, IN WHICH CASE I WON'T!

SO, I GOT CONFUSED AND WALKED AWAY.

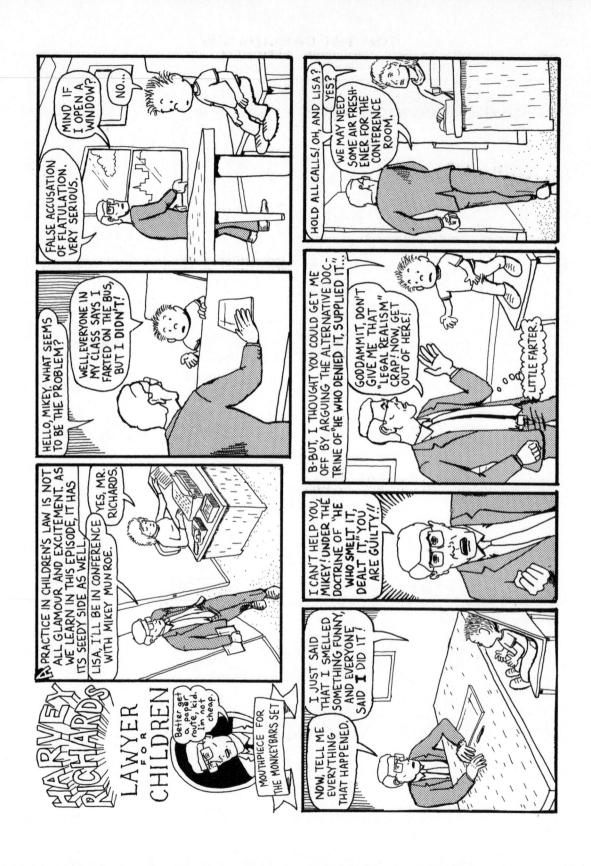

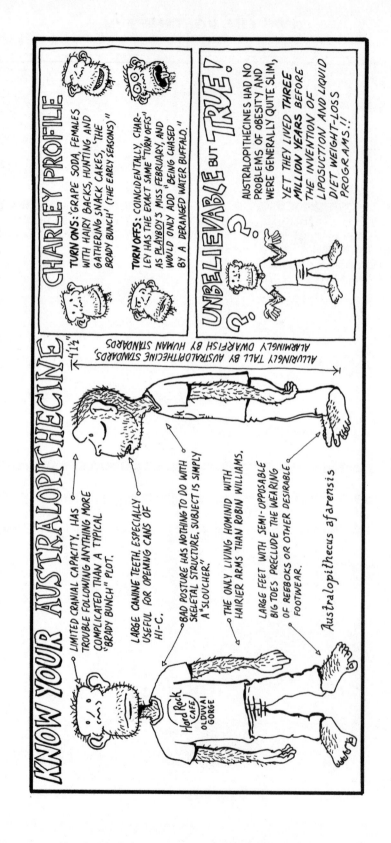

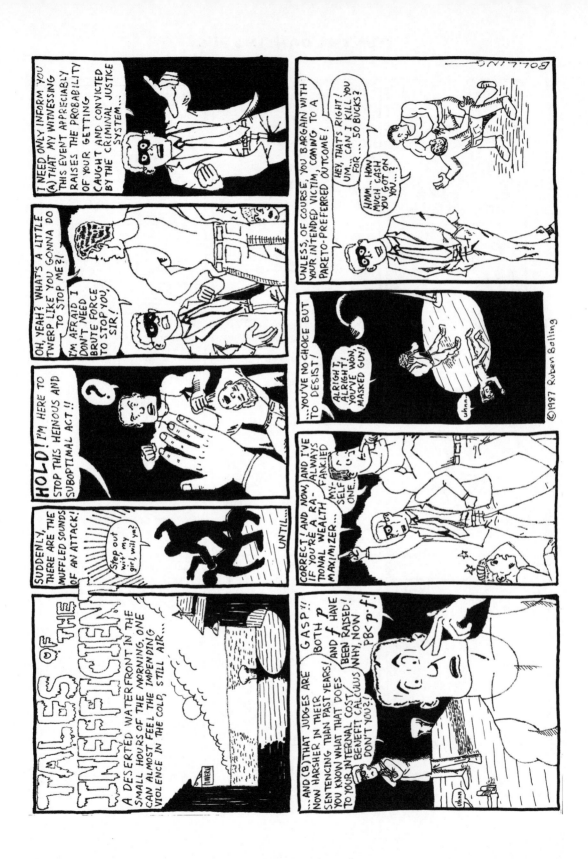

HEY, KIDS! GOT TROUBLE WITH PARENTS? **WHO DOESN'T?**

AN ATTORNEY SPECIALIZING IN CHILDREN'S LAW NOW OFFERS A TREATISE ON DEALING WITH PARENTS--

RICHARDS ON PARENTS

HARVEY RICHARDS, ESQ. "LAWYER FOR CHILDREN"

I CAN HAVE YOU *WINNING ARGUMENTS* WITH YOUR PARENTS WITHIN DAYS!

HOW MANY TIMES HAS THIS PARENTAL ARGUMENT STUMPED YOU?

WHY NOT?

BECAUSE I SAID SO!

OH.

IMAGINE YOUR PARENTS' REACTION WHEN YOU RESPOND:

"THAT'S THE KIND OF DESPOTIC DECREE THAT IS NOT ONLY ANATHEMA TO ALL FREE-THINKING PEOPLE, IT IS ALSO LIKELY TO CULTIVATE A RESENTMENT TOWARD AUTHORITY THAT WILL IMPAIR MY SOCIAL ADVANCEMENT."

JUST MEMORIZE A FEW PASSAGES FROM MY BOOK, AND YOU'LL EASILY COUNTER THOSE IRRATIONAL BANALITIES PARENTS ALWAYS USE.

FOR EXAMPLE, IF YOUR PARENTS SAY:

IF YOUR FRIENDS JUMPED OFF THE EMPIRE STATE BUILDING, WOULD IT BE OKAY FOR YOU TO?

YOU REPLY:

"TO EQUATE LEAPING OFF A TALL EDIFICE WITH [HAVING MY EARS PIERCED] IS TO ENGAGE IN HYPERBOLIC ARGUMENTATION WHICH IS FAR MORE INFLAMMATORY THAN ILLUMINATIVE."

OR DOES THIS EXCHANGE SOUND FAMILIAR?

THAT'S NOT *FAIR!*

WELL, *LIFE* ISN'T FAIR

SIMPLY ANSWER:

"PERHAPS NOT, BUT IF WE GIVE UP THE STRUGGLE TO MAKE IT AS FAIR AS WE CAN, THEN SURELY WE ARE GIVING IN TO THE FORCES OF INEQUITY THAT WE PROFESS TO ABHOR."

I GUARANTEE YOUR PARENTS WILL LET YOU HAVE THE RUN OF THE HOUSE--JUST TO **SHUT YOU UP!**

Games Louis Plays.

Thoughts of a Rightfielder.

INSPIRED BY THE COMEBACK OF DAVID CASSIDY, ANOTHER FORMER MEMBER OF "THE PARTRIDGE FAMILY" TAKES A STAB AT MUSICAL STARDOM.

NOW APPEARING at the BULLPEN: ☆ Brian ☆ ☆ Forster ☆ formerly "CHRIS PARTRIDGE" drummer of TV's "The Partridge Family"

UNFORTUNATELY, THE RESPONSE TO HIS EFFORTS IS TEPID.

AFTER THE SHOW...

SORRY, FORSTER, I'M LETTIN' YA GO.

WHAT?! I'M JUST HITTING MY STRIDE!

NAW, KID, THERE'S ONLY SO FAR NOSTALGIA CAN GO. AN ALL-PERCUSSION VERSION OF "I WOKE UP IN LOVE THIS MORNING" IS WAY, **WAY** TOO FAR.

YOU BASTARD!! EX-CHILD STARS CAN'T CATCH A BREAK! AT LEAST I'M NOT ON DRUGS OR KNOCKING OFF LIQUOR STORES!

YEAH, YEAH. PICK UP YOUR TAKE AT THE CASHIER.

A BITTER BRIAN FORSTER RETURNS TO HIS APARTMENT.

THE ACT JUST NEEDS ONE MORE ELEMENT TO PUSH IT OVER THE EDGE.

SUDDENLY, INSPIRATION HITS HIM.

HI, SUZANNE? IT'S ME -- BRIAN!! LISTEN, YOU STILL PLAY THE TAMBOURINE?

AND BRIAN IS BACK ON HIS COMEBACK TRAIL!

Now Appearing at the BREW OR 2 BRIAN FORSTER with SUZANNE CROUGH The Partridge Family's CHRIS & TRACY

HOW TO CHOOSE A SUPREME COURT JUSTICE

FIRST YOU NEED TO DEFINE YOUR QUALIFICATIONS.

FOR EXAMPLE, LET'S SAY YOU NEED A HISPANIC, FEMALE, HANDICAPPED, SOMEWHAT RELIGIOUS, VERY CONSERVATIVE 51-YEAR-OLD STRICT CONSTRUCTIONIST WHO HAS NEVER SMOKED MARIJUANA.

ONLY EIGHT SUCH PEOPLE EXIST.

UNFORTUNATELY, NONE OF THEM HAVE LAW DEGREES.

BUT WE'RE IN LUCK! ONE WORKED BRIEFLY AS A FILE CLERK IN THE TULSA, OKLA. BUREAU OF TRAFFIC ADJUDICATIONS!

RIOS, JULIA

WE HAVE OUR JUSTICE!!

NOW WE NEED TO WEATHER THE PRESS FOR THE NEXT FEW WEEKS.

THE COMPARISONS:

HACKENSACK GAZETTE
RITA SANCHEZ PASSED OVER
Federal Appeals Judge for 20 years: Ignored

TARZANA POST
WHY NOT WILLIAM SIMMONS?
Vision-Impaired Professor of Law at Stanford

DREDGING UP THE PAST-- EVEN THE MOST CAREFULLY CHOSEN NOMINEE WILL HAVE *SOME* PAPER TRAIL:

TAMPA-LEDGER
RIOS'S 1974 LETTER TO EDITOR: "I HATE PUPPIES"!
Rios   A puppy

THE OSHKOSH JOURNAL
Possible Clues to Rios's Stand on Abortion in 7th Grade History Paper Recently Discovered.
Rios at 13.

HAVE THE BIG GUY ISSUE A FIRM STATEMENT.

THE FACT THAT MS. RIOS IS A HISPANIC, FEMALE, HANDICAPPED, SOMEWHAT RELIGIOUS, VERY CONSERVATIVE 51-YEAR-OLD STRICT CONSTRUCTIONIST WHO HAS NEVER SMOKED MARIJUANA HAD **NOTHING** TO DO WITH MY DECISION TO NOMINATE HER.

PREPARE YOUR NOMINEE TO BE RESPECTFULLY EVASIVE AT THE CONFIRMATION HEARINGS.

IT WOULD BE IMPRUDENT TO COMMENT ON HYPOTHETICAL CASES...

AND WE'VE GOT ANOTHER MEMBER OF THE NATION'S HIGHEST COURT!

RIGHTS, SHMIGHTS! THIS GUY'S A WHINING CRYBABY PURE AND SIMPLE!

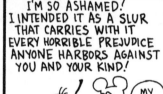

Remember when a summer was a virtual eternity? When it seemed a Saturday was enough time to accomplish almost anything? When years didn't flick by like shuffling cards? What happened?

It's just another alarming aspect of the aging process-- our plummet through time is **ACCELERATING!** Let's look at the subjective passage of **ONE HOUR** as an individual grows older...

At age five, an hour is a huge chunk of time, which will include a range of experiences and emotions.

At age fifteen, an hour is still substantial, but you've come to learn it will pass quickly enough.

By age twenty-five, an hour has become an almost negligible unit of time.

At this rate of acceleration, it's easy to see why elderly folk seem so sedentary.

LET'S SEE IF WE CAN FIND THE **ONE WORD** THAT CAN
MAKE DOUG MAD!

THERE'S BEEN A LOT OF CONFUSION RECENTLY ABOUT MORAL BEHAVIOR. IT'S ACTUALLY A MATTER OF ONE SIMPLE RULE: *THE MORE A LIVING BEING IS LIKE YOU, THE NICER YOU MUST BE TO IT.* CARRY AROUND THIS HANDY CHART, CONSULT IT AS YOU COME ACROSS ORGANISMS, AND ACT ACCORDINGLY.

HUMAN MORALITY
MADE SIMPLE

KEY
Y = YES, ALWAYS
S = SOMETIMES, DEPENDING ON CIRCUMSTANCES
M = IF YOU'RE IN THE MOOD
N = NO, NEVER

CATEGORY	EXAMPLE	HOW MUCH LIKE YOU?	APPROPRIATE MORAL RESPONSE	SHOULD YOU HELP IT?	CAN YOU HARM IT?	CAN YOU KILL IT?	CAN YOU EAT IT?
IMMEDIATE FAMILY MEMBERS	DAUGHTER	ALMOST EXACTLY LIKE YOU	MUST BE UNBELIEVABLY NICE AND GENEROUS. GIVE IT MONEY. DEVOTE YOUR LIFE TO ITS WELL-BEING	Y	N	N	N
EXTENDED FAMILY MEMBERS, FRIENDS	COUSIN	VERY MUCH LIKE YOU.	MUST BE VERY KIND. HELP IT IF NOT TOO COSTLY TO YOURSELF. MAKE SURE NEVER TO HARM IT.	S	N	N	N
COMMUNITY MEMBERS	FELLOW AMERICAN	SAME CUSTOMS, VALUE SYSTEM, T.V. SHOWS	MAY ONLY HARM IF YOU CAN GAIN BY IT (EG. IN BUSINESS DEALS). NO NEED TO HELP IT. NOTE: THIS LINE NEED NOT BE DRAWN GEO-POLITICALLY ONLY. FOR EXAMPLE, IF YOU VIEW YOUR RACIAL GROUP AS YOUR "COMMUNITY," DROP MEMBERS OF OTHER RACES TO "OUTSIDER" STATUS.	M	S	N	N
OUTSIDERS	FOREIGNER	LOOKS DIFFERENT, ACTS WEIRD	CAN BE MEAN TO, IF NECESSARY. MAY KILL, IF WARTIME.	M	S	S	N
PETS AND PRIMATES	DOG	NOT HUMAN, BUT ANTHROPO-MORPHIZED	CAN HARM, IF FOR RESEARCH. CAN PUT IT TO SLEEP, IF NECESSARY. CAN'T EAT IT.	M	S	S	N
OTHER MAMMALS	DEER	DIFFERENT	CAN KILL, CAN EAT. PAT IT ON THE HEAD.	M	S	Y	Y
OTHER ANIMALS	FISH	VERY DIFFERENT	CAN KILL, CAN EAT. DON'T PAT IT ON THE HEAD.	N	Y	Y	Y
INVERTEBRATES	LADYBUG	GROSSLY DIFFERENT	STOMP ON IT, FEEL A LITTLE GUILTY.	N	Y	Y	YECH
PLANTS	RADISH	ABSOLUTELY DIFFERENT	DESTROY WITHOUT A TWINGE OF GUILT.	N	Y	Y	Y

♪ HEY IT'S MAX AND DOUG, EVERYONE'S FAVORITE PAIR, FROM "TOM THE DANCING BUG," THEY'RE THE TEAM WITH SAVOIR FAIRE! ♪

♪ THEY'RE FUNNY--WHAT A HOOT, A KNEE-SLAPPIN' SIDE-SPLITTER, WHAT COULD BE AS CUTE, AS A BABY AND A CRITTER?! ♪

♪ OH, MAX IS SUCH A RIOT, WHEN FOX-HUNTING HE YELLS "YOIK", AND DOUG WILL DENY IT, BUT HE'S REALLY JUST A **DOIK**! ♪

♪ A DOIK, A DOIK, A DOIK, DOUG SURE IS A DOIK... YE- ♪

STOP THE MUSIC!

WHAT'S WRONG?

THAT WORD!! THAT WORD CAN'T BE IN OUR THEME SONG!!

DON'T BE SO SENSITIVE. IT'S JUST A SILLY WORD.

IT'S A *SLUR* THAT I FIND PERSONALLY AND DEEPLY OFFENSIVE!

IT JUST HAPPENED TO FIT INTO THE SONG!

I'LL THANK YOU **NEVER** TO USE THAT WORD AGAIN!

"WHEN FOX-HUNTING HE YELLS YOIK"?!!

YOU TRY TO RHYME DO-

HEY!

HEY, KIDS!

THERE ARE HUNDREDS OF BOOKS ADVISING PARENTS HOW TO HANDLE CHILDREN. FINALLY, AN ATTORNEY SPECIALIZING IN CHILDREN'S LAW OFFERS:

RICHARDS ON PARENTS

HARVEY RICHARDS, ESQ. "LAWYER FOR CHILDREN"

A TREATISE ADVISING CHILDREN ON HOW TO DEAL WITH PARENTAL AUTHORITY IN A LEGALLY SOPHISTICATED MANNER.

MY BOOK WILL SHOW YOU HOW TO UTILIZE THE "**EXACT WORDS**" DOCTRINE[1] TO *MINIMIZE* OR *NEGATE* THE EFFECT OF ANY PUNISHMENT OR RESTRICTION.

[1] See, eg., Greg Brady, Brady Bunch, Episode 107.

FOR EXAMPLE, IS YOUR PUNISHMENT THAT YOU "CAN'T WATCH T.V."? YOUR PARENTS DIDN'T SAY ANYTHING ABOUT WATCHING A **MIRROR** AND **LISTENING** TO T.V.!

AND NOW, BACK TO OUR PROGRAM!

YOUR PARENTS ARE ALWAYS TELLING YOU TO LISTEN TO THEM. WELL, YOU **SHOULD** -- *VERY CAREFULLY!* DID THEY SAY YOU COULDN'T "TOUCH" ANY SNACKS UNTIL AFTER DINNER?

Chips Aplenty

WITH THOUGHTFUL PLANNING, ALMOST ANY RULE CAN BE CIRCUMVENTED.

I WASN'T RUNNING. I WAS GALLOPING!

OF COURSE, THIS STRATEGY MAY CAUSE YOUR PARENTS TO START GIVING DIRECTIONS WITH SUFFICIENT SPECIFICITY. IN THAT CASE, YOU MAY WANT TO CALL IN A PROFESSIONAL LIKE MYSELF.

... SHALL NOT PLAY NINTENDO, SUPER-NINTENDO OR ANY OTHER VIDEO-BASED AMUSEMENTS UNTIL "HOMEWORK", AS DEFINED IN...

I BELIEVE "HOMEWORK" IS DEFINED IN §13.5

Thanx to Seeds!

NATURAL SELECTION AT WORK

2 GENERATIONS LATER:

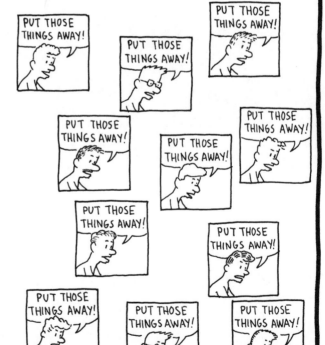

CLARENCE T.'s KAFKAESQUE NIGHTMARE

Hey, Kids! Wise Up!

IT'S TIME YOU STARTED TAKING A MORE INTELLIGENT APPROACH TO DEALING WITH YOUR PARENTS.

THIS BOOK WILL SHOW YOU HOW!

RICHARDS ON PARENTS

HARVEY RICHARDS, ESQ "LAWYER FOR CHILDREN"

MR. HARVEY RICHARDS:

YOUR PARENTS CARE VERY DEEPLY ABOUT YOUR HAPPINESS AND WELL-BEING. *YOU CAN USE THIS AGAINST THEM!*

LET'S SAY THERE'S SOMETHING YOU'D LIKE OF YOUR PARENTS...

THE TRADITIONAL METHODS ARE REMARKABLY INEFFECTIVE.

CAN I HAVE A SUPER-PALS-DELUXE-ACTION-FIGURES-HEADQUARTERS-GIFT-SET?

NO!

KIDS FROM TIME IMMEMORIAL HAVE USED THIS TECHNIQUE WITH VIRTUALLY NO SUCCESS.

I WANT IT! I WANT IT!

MY BOOK WILL INTRODUCE YOU TO A MORE SOPHISTICATED APPROACH TO THIS PROBLEM.

BEGIN BY SULKING AROUND THE HOUSE FOR A FEW DAYS.

IS SOMETHING BOTHERING YOU, JOHNNY?

NO...

KEEP IT UP. ACT SAD A COUPLE MORE DAYS. EAT A BIT LESS.

WHAT'S THE MATTER?

NOTHIN'

BE PERSISTENT.

COME ON JOHNNY... TELL US.

NOT YET.

SIGH

ONE MORE DAY.

JOHNNY! PLEASE! WHAT'S WRONG?!

NOW.

WELL, MAYBE IF I HAD A SUPER-PALS-DELUXE-ACTION-FIGURES-HEADQUARTERS-GIFT-SET...

YOUR PARENTS WILL NEVER SUSPECT THIS KIND OF FORESIGHT AND DUPLICITY FROM A KID --YOU'LL BE SURPRISED AT THE KIND OF POWER YOU CAN WIELD.

Max & Doug Discuss the Oscar-nominated Movies

FIRST--"JFK." AN EXCELLENT MOVIE! I LEARNED SO MUCH!

I KNEW THE CONSPIRACY WAS EXTENSIVE, BUT WHEN I SAW THAT LOU GRANT WAS INVOLVED, I WAS FLOORED!

THE FAT GUY

THE BALD GUY

"BEAUTY AND THE BEAST"-- TOTALLY UNREALISTIC! GIVE ME A BREAK!

I KNOW! "JFK" PRESENTED A MUCH MORE CREDIBLE HYPOTHESIS!

I LIKED "BUGSY." IT SHOWED A BASICALLY GOOD GUY WHO HAD SOME FLAWS.

YUP. A COMPLEX CHARACTER STUDY. ON THE ONE HAND, HE KILLED PEOPLE. ON THE OTHER, HE THOUGHT OF LAS VEGAS. WHO'S TO SAY?

"PRINCE OF TIDES." WOW! AN EMOTIONAL UPHEAVAL!

ESPECIALLY THE SCENE WHEN MIKE WALLACE STARTED IN ON HER.

OH! AND HOW ABOUT THE PART WHERE THE ACADEMY IGNORES AND MISUNDERSTANDS HER!

I WEPT OPENLY!

ALRIGHT. "SILENCE OF THE LAMBS."

JODIE FOSTER HAS GOTTEN A LOT OF CREDIT FOR PORTRAYING STRONG WOMEN, CHALLENGING THE FILM STEREOTYPE.

UNFORTUNATELY, THIS MOVIE HAPPENED TO REINFORCE EVERY NEGATIVE AND EVEN HORRIFIC STEREOTYPE ABOUT HOMOSEXUALS!

OKAY, SO IT'S A WASH.

OUR PREDICTION FOR THE WINNER... THE ZAPRUDER FILM!

UNLESS CUOMO JUMPS IN AT THE LAST MINUTE.

THANK YOU! YOU'VE BEEN GREAT.

WE REJOIN BRIAN FORSTER AS HE STRUGGLES TO REGAIN THE FLEETING STARDOM HE ENJOYED AS AN 8-YEAR-OLD MEMBER OF "THE PARTRIDGE FAMILY."

"THE 'PIZZA PALACE' PRESENTS THE DRUMMING MAGIC OF BRIAN FORSTER."

ALRIGHT! CHRIS PARTRIDGE *LIVES*!!

REST ROO...

BUT HIS LESS-THAN-METEORIC RISE IS SUDDENLY PUT IN JEOPARDY!

NEXT UP: REMEMBER CUTE CHRIS PARTRIDGE? WELL, HE'S GROWN UP AND IN TROUBLE WITH THE LAW! JEREMY GELBWAKS!

WHAT?!

BRIAN IMMEDIATELY SEEKS LEGAL COUNSEL.

HE ONLY PLAYED CHRIS PARTRIDGE FOR ONE SEASON! *I* PUT IN *4 YEARS* AS AMERICA'S FAVORITE DRUMMER BOY!!

THERE'S NOTHING YOU CAN DO, BRIAN.

I WORK HARD TO DEVELOP MY CRAFT AND I GET SQUAT! HE PUNCHES OUT A COP AND HE GETS ON OPRAH!

A MEETING IS ARRANGED.

I CAN'T HAVE YOU GOING AROUND CLAIMING TO BE CHRIS PARTRIDGE!

HEY, PAL! I WAS THE ORIGINAL AND THE BEST!

BUT HOSTILITIES SOON GIVE WAY TO SHARED MEMORIES.

...AND DAVE MADDEN! MAN, HIS BREATH STANK!

THE WORST! SMELLED LIKE THERE WAS A ROTTING 'POSSUM IN HIS GUT!

AND AN ALLIANCE IS FORMED THAT WILL FOREVER CHANGE THE WAY THE WORLD THINKS OF CHRIS PARTRIDGE.

ARENA OFF EXIT 4A

Giant WHEELS of DEATH

plus BOTH CHRIS PARTRIDGES in "DUELLING DRUMS"!

MOST PEOPLE WOULD AGREE THAT THE "SURGEON GENERAL'S WARNING" BOXES THAT ARE REQUIRED ON CIGARETTE ADS ARE WHOLLY INEFFECTIVE. YOU CAN'T COUNTER A VISUALLY-STIMULATING IMAGE WITH A SENTENCE RATIONALLY IMPARTING SCIENTIFIC INFORMATION. THESE BOXES SHOULD APPEAL TO PEOPLE ON THE SAME EMOTIONAL LEVEL AS THE ADS. HERE ARE A FEW EXAMPLES.

EFFECTIVE CIGARETTE WARNINGS

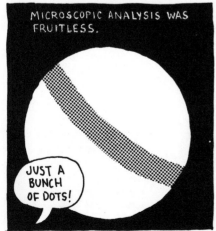

HARVEY RICHARDS
LAWYER FOR CHILDREN

A FREE BALLOON WITH EVERY CONSULTATION

MR. RICHARDS WAS IN A MEETING WHEN...

I'M SORRY, BRIAN. I DON'T GIVE KOOTY SHOTS...

EXCUSE ME. RANDY GORDON IS ON LINE TWO. HE SAYS IT'S AN EMERGENCY.

WHAT'S THE PROBLEM, RANDY?

WELL, I WAS ON THE SWINGS, AND SUDDENLY THESE GUYS SAID, "LAST ONE TO THE SEE-SAW GETS SHOULDER SLUGS FROM EVERYONE!"

AND YOU WERE LAST, HM? SOUNDS PAINFUL.

YEAH! WHAT CAN I DO?!

QUICK-- CALL "NOT INCLUDED"!

BUT THEY ALREADY CALLED "EVERYBODY INCLUDED"!

PRETTY CLEVER, BUT NO PROBLEM! JUST CALL "EXCEPT ME"!

NO WAY, MR. RICHARDS! WE ALREADY CALLED "NO EXCEPT-ME'S"!

OH, NO! THAT CAN ONLY MEAN ONE THING...

THAT'S RIGHT, RICHARDS! YOU'VE GOT OPPOSING COUNSEL!

EDWARD POTTER
LAWYER FOR CHILDREN

A FREE BALLOON AND LOLLIPOP WITH EVERY CONSULTATION

I HOPE YOU'VE GOT A FULL PIGGY BANK, RANDY. THIS IS GOING TO GET EXPENSIVE!

Next: PULSE-POUNDING PLAYGROUND PROCEEDINGS

HARVEY RICHARDS LAWYER FOR CHILDREN

A FREE BALLOON WITH EVERY CONSULTATION

WHEN WE LAST SAW MR. RICHARDS, HE WAS EMBROILED IN A LEGAL BATTLE WITH HIS NEMESIS, EDWARD POTTER!

MY CLIENT ISN'T TAKING ONE SHOULDER-SLUG, POTTER!

THEN, YOU'D BETTER START SOME FAST TALKING, RICHARDS! MY CLIENTS CALLED, "LAST ONE TO THE SEE-SAW GETS SHOULDER-SLUGS FROM EVERYONE"!

THEY ALSO CALLED "EVERYONE INCLUDED" AND NO "EXCEPT-ME"'S.

HMM... BUT YOU DIDN'T SAY WHICH SEE-SAW SET! THERE'S ONE ACROSS TOWN...

WHAT-- YOU THINK I'M AN AMATEUR?! I'D DRAFTED THIS DOCUMENT FULLY SPECIFYING THIS LOCATION!

BUT YOU DIDN'T CALL WHEN THE RACE STARTS...

"STARTING THEN"!

"STARTING LATER"!

HA! I GOT IT IN FIRST! WE'VE GOT AN AIR-TIGHT CASE NOW, RICHARDS!

DAMN!

I'M AFRAID HE'S RIGHT, RANDY. YOU'LL HAVE TO TAKE THOSE SHOULDER-SLUGS.

WHAT?!

WANT TO GRAB A BEER, POTTER?

SURE, I'VE GOT SOME TIME BEFORE MY 3:00...

AUGH! MR. RICHARDS!

POW POW

Games Louis Plays. What if I got one wish?

MY ONE WISH WOULD BE FOR...

INFINITY *MORE* WISHES!

EXCEPT THEN WHAT IF I ACCIDENTALLY WISHED FOR SOMETHING HORRIBLE?

I WISH THEY WERE DE... WHOOPS!!

POP   POP

MOM   DAD

I COULD WISH THAT I NEVER WISHED THAT, BUT THAT WOULD BE REALLY WEIRD!

WE'RE BACK!

YEAH, IF I WAS ALWAYS WISHING STUFF-- I'D HATE THAT! IT'S LIKE THERE WOULD BE NO REALITY!

HEY, LOUIS! WE NEED YOU TO PLAY SHORTSTOP!

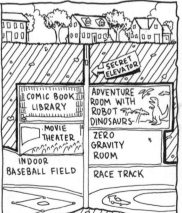

OKAY, SO I'D MAKE IT SO I ONLY HAVE ONE WISH A WEEK, SO THAT I COULD HAVE TIME TO THINK OF REALLY COOL STUFF THAT WOULDN'T HURT REALITY MUCH.

SECRET ELEVATOR

COMIC BOOK LIBRARY

ADVENTURE ROOM WITH ROBOT DINOSAURS

MOVIE THEATER

ZERO GRAVITY ROOM

INDOOR BASEBALL FIELD

RACE TRACK

I'M GLAD I WORKED THAT OUT!

NEWS OF THE TIMES

🎺

MRS. IRENE HELMINGER REVOLUTIONIZES SCIENTIFIC THOUGHT

MRS. HELMINGER'S AMAZING STORY HAS SHOCKED PHYSICISTS AND PHILOSOPHERS ALIKE.

WELL, I WAS TALKING TO MY SISTER-IN-LAW, BETTY, AND I KEPT MENTIONING THAT "LOVE BOAT" SHOW. ANYWAY, THAT NIGHT, I LOOK AT THE TV GUIDE, AND *GUESS WHO'S* ON THE TONIGHT SHOW -- GAVIN MacLEOD!

DR. CRUFTSEN OF CAMBRIDGE UNIVERSITY EXPLAINS THE PROFOUND SIGNIFICANCE OF MRS. HELMINGER'S REVELATION.

MRS. HELMINGER'S STORY PROVES BEYOND ANY DOUBT THAT THERE IS, IN FACT, ORDER TO THE **UNIVERSE!**

THE WORLD'S INTELLECTUAL COMMUNITY IS TURNED ON ITS EAR. DR. PERSKARSKY OF CORNELL UNIVERSITY:

ALL OF **MY** THEORIES, PREMISED ON THE TENET THAT THE UNIVERSE IS A CHAOTIC SYSTEM OF RANDOM EVENTS, ARE RENDERED WORTHLESS FECES.

MRS. HELMINGER'S NOW-HISTORIC SPEECH AT NOBEL PRIZE CEREMONIES IS AT FIRST HUMBLE...

I THOUGHT IT WAS AN INTERESTING STORY. I DIDN'T KNOW SUCH A FUSS WOULD BE MADE.

...THEN SHE STUNS THE CROWD WITH YET ANOTHER DOGMA-CRUMBLING ACCOUNT.

I MEAN, THIS HAPPENS TO ME ALL THE TIME! IT'S LIKE THE TIME I MEANT TO CALL RITA HODGSON, BUT I DIALED LINDA SCHMIDT BY ACCIDENT... AND RITA WAS **AT** LINDA'S!

ARGG! GASP! GASP!

ABOUT THE AUTHOR

Ruben Bolling (born: 1908, Prague) began "Tom the Dancing Bug" in the campus newspaper while he was attending law school. The comic strip proved to be an immediate success, with many of the words from the title becoming campus buzzwords (particularly "the"). After graduation, he continued the comic strip, and it now appears in newspapers across the country, not including the *New York Times*, *USA Today*, and *Women's Wear Daily*.

Bolling now resides in New York City with his wife and two turtles. In his spare time he enjoys crochet, word-find puzzles, and sky-surfing. When not in his spare time, he abhors these activities. He also practices law, and does not have a favorite color.